WOULD RATHER
BOOK FOR KIDS
AGES 7-13
BY J. FABIAN RAMA

THE ILLUSTRATIONS WERE MADE BY AGNES RAMA

THE RULES OF THE GAME

Would you Rather be a fun game that consists of 10 rounds
Each round contains 20 questions.
A minimum of two players is required for this game, but the number of players can be unlimited, the more people the fun can be crazier and more attractive to players.
 Player number 1 starts round one and player number 2 asks questions.
If there is a greater number of people, everyone can join the player of their choice.
The scoring scale is 1-10.
The number of points depends on the weirdest, stupid or insane answer. The evaluation of this answer is given by the player from the opposing team or his group.
 If player number 1 finishes the round, player number 2 starts the next round
(scoring remains unchanged).
The winner is the player or group of players who scores the most points in the entire game.
The prize for winning the game is a super cup, but the bigger reward is your child's smile and fun.
If the match ends in a draw, both teams win.
Would You Rather.
It can be played by parents with children, grandparents with grandchildren, or siblings.

TABLE OF CONTENTS

ROUND 1
SILLY QUESTIONS   P. 1

ROUND 2
FUNNY QUESTIONS   P. 13

ROUND 3
ANIMAL QUESTIONS   P. 25

ROUND 4
HOLIDAY QUESTIONS   P. 37

ROUND 5
CHALLENGING QUESTIONS P. 49

ROUND 6
HILARIOUS QUESTIONS   P. 61

ROUND 7
HARDEST QUESTIONS   P. 73

ROUND 8
GROSS QUESTIONS   P. 85

ROUND 9
SPORTS QUESTIONS   P. 97

ROUND 10
FOOD QUESTIONS   P. 109

A SPECIAL BONUS OF 56
KNOCK-KNOCK JOKES   P. 121

WOULD YOU RATHER?

ROUND 1
SILLY
QUESTIONS

PLAYER NUMBER 1 STARTS THE GAME

WOULD YOU RATHER

EAT THE WORST FOOD IN THE WORLD

HEAR THE WORST SOUND IN THE WORLD?

Q1

POINTS: _____ 1/10

WOULD YOU RATHER

LIVE IN A HOUSE FULL OF CHEESE

CHOCOLATE?

Q2

POINTS: _____ 1/10

WOULD YOU RATHER

RIDE A FLYING BUS

RIDE A UNICORN?

POINTS: _____1/10

WOULD YOU RATHER

LIVE IN THE CLOUDS

UNDERWATER?

POINTS: _____1/10

WOULD YOU RATHER

HAVE A MONKEY'S TAIL

AN ELEPHANT'S TRUNK?

Q/5

POINTS: _____1/10

WOULD YOU RATHER

BE THE SMARTEST PERSON

THE FUNNIEST?

Q/6

POINTS: _____1/10

WOULD YOU RATHER

NEVER EAT DESSERT

NEVER SLEEP?

POINTS: _____1/10

WOULD YOU RATHER

FLY TO THE MOON

BE INVISIBLE?

POINTS: _____1/10

WOULD YOU RATHER

HAVE A MILLION DOLLARS

A MILLION FRIENDS?

POINTS: _____1/10

WOULD YOU RATHER

SING LIKE A CHICKEN

WADDLE LIKE A PENGUIN?

POINTS: _____1/10

WOULD YOU RATHER

HAVE PURPLE SKIN

A BLUE TONGUE?

POINTS: _____ 1/10

WOULD YOU RATHER

NOT BE ABLE TO TASTE ANYTHING

FEEL ANYTHING?

POINTS: _____ 1/10

WOULD YOU RATHER

BE AS QUIET AS A MOUSE

AS LOUD AS A LION?

POINTS: _____ I/10

WOULD YOU RATHER

BE AS TINY AS A FLY

AS BIG AS A WHALE?

POINTS: _____ I/10

WOULD YOU RATHER

LIVE IN A SHOE

A TREE?

POINTS: _____ I/10

WOULD YOU RATHER

HAVE 100 BROTHERS

100 PETS?

POINTS: _____ I/10

WOULD YOU RATHER

SLIDE DOWN A RAINBOW

JUMP ON A CLOUD?

POINTS: _____1/10

WOULD YOU RATHER

SLIDE DOWN A RAINBOW

JUMP ON A CLOUD?

POINTS: _____1/10

WOULD YOU RATHER

EAT WEIRD FOOD

WEAR WEIRD CLOTHES?

POINTS: _____ /10

WOULD YOU RATHER

SPLASH IN PUDDLES

MUD?

POINTS: _____ /10

END OF THE FIRST ROUND

PLAYER NUMBER 1'S POINTS SCORED

POINTS ....

WOULD YOU RATHER?

ROUND 2
FUNNY
QUESTIONS

PLAYER 2 STARTS THE GAME

WOULD YOU RATHER

HAVE THREE ARMS

THREE EYES?

Q/1   POINTS: _____1/10

WOULD YOU RATHER

EAT A SPOONFUL OF MUSTARD

A SPOONFUL OF MAYONNAISE?

Q/2   POINTS: _____1/10

WOULD YOU RATHER

LIVE IN A DIFFERENT COUNTRY

LIVE ON A DIFFERENT PLANET?

Q/3

POINTS: _____1/10

WOULD YOU RATHER

MEET AN ALIEN

MEET A MYTHICAL CREATURE?

Q/4

POINTS: _____1/10

WOULD YOU RATHER

STEP ON A LEGO

GET A TOY HELICOPTER STUCK IN YOUR HAIR?

POINTS: _____ I/10

WOULD YOU RATHER

GET GUM STUCK IN YOUR HAIR

CORN STUCK IN YOUR TEETH?

POINTS: _____ I/10

WOULD YOU RATHER

STAY HOME FOR 30 DAYS STRAIGHT

STAY AT SCHOOL WITH YOUR FRIENDS AND TEACHERS FOR 30 DAYS STRAIGHT?

Q/7

POINTS: _____1/10

WOULD YOU RATHER

HAVE 15 SIBLINGS

15 PETS?

Q/8

POINTS: _____1/10

WOULD YOU RATHER

HAVE NO EYEBROWS

NO TEETH?

POINTS: _____1/10

WOULD YOU RATHER

BE ALLERGIC TO YOUR FAVORITE FOOD

ALLERGIC TO YOUR FAVORITE ANIMAL?

POINTS: _____1/10

WOULD YOU RATHER

HAVE TO EAT FOOD THAT YOU HATE EVERY DAY

OR

LISTEN TO A SONG THAT YOU HATE EVERY DAY?

Q 11

POINTS: _____ /10

WOULD YOU RATHER

HAVE WITCH NAILS

OR

ALIEN SKIN?

Q 12

POINTS: _____ /10

WOULD YOU RATHER

HAVE LUNCH WITH A CANNIBAL

GET ABDUCTED BY FASHION-FORWARD ALIENS?

POINTS: _____ 1/10

WOULD YOU RATHER

SPEND THE REST OF YOUR LIFE WATCHING HARRY POTTER

READING HARRY POTTER?

POINTS: _____ 1/10

WOULD YOU RATHER

BE STUCK IN A LOCKED CAGE WITH AN ENEMY

A RAGING BULL?

POINTS: _____I/10

WOULD YOU RATHER

SLEEP IN AN OPEN GRAVE

A CAGE AT THE ZOO?

POINTS: _____I/10

WOULD YOU RATHER

BE TEN INCHES

TEN FEET TALL?

Q/17

POINTS: _____ 1/10

WOULD YOU RATHER

IT THUNDERS EVERY TIME YOU WENT TO THE BATHROOM

IT RAIN ANY TIME YOU SPOKE?

Q/18

POINTS: _____ 1/10

WOULD YOU RATHER

EAT LUNCH OFF A LEPRECHAUN'S STOMACH

GO SWIMMING IN SHARK-INFESTED WATERS?

POINTS: _____ /10

WOULD YOU RATHER

EAT BUGS

CAT FOOD FOR THE REST OF YOUR LIFE?

POINTS: _____ /10

END OF ROUND TWO

PLAYER NUMBER 2'S POINTS SCORED

POINTS ....

WOULD YOU RATHER?

ROUND 3
ANIMAL
QUESTIONS

PLAYER 1 STARTS THE THIRD ROUND

WOULD YOU RATHER

LICK A FROG

EAT A BUG?

POINTS: _____ 1/10

WOULD YOU RATHER

RUN LIKE A JAGUAR, SWIM LIKE A PENGUIN

FLY LIKE A BIRD?

POINTS: _____ 1/10

WOULD YOU RATHER

HAVE THE EARS OF A BUNNY

THE EYES OF A COW?

POINTS: _____I/IO

WOULD YOU RATHER

EAT GARBAGE LIKE A BEAR

SLOP LIKE A PIG?

POINTS: _____I/IO

WOULD YOU RATHER

BE RAISED BY OWLS

RAISED BY MONKEYS?

Q/5　　　　　　　　POINTS: _____ I/10

WOULD YOU RATHER

Q/6　　　　　　　　POINTS: _____ I/10

WOULD YOU RATHER

MIGRATE SOUTH FOR THE WINTER

HIBERNATE ALL WINTER?

POINTS: _____ 1/10

WOULD YOU RATHER

HAVE SNAKE SCALES

DUCK FEATHERS?

POINTS: _____ 1/10

WOULD YOU RATHER

HAVE A HEDGEHOG AS A PET

A TEACUP PIG AS A PET?

Q/9

POINTS: _____1/10

WOULD YOU RATHER

HAVE AN ELEPHANT THAT'S AS SMALL AS A CAT

A GOAT THAT'S AS SMALL AS A HAMSTER?

Q/10

POINTS: _____1/10

WOULD YOU RATHER

RIDE A CAMEL

RIDE A LLAMA?

POINTS: _____ I/10

WOULD YOU RATHER

BE WOKEN UP EARLY EVERY DAY BY A ROOSTER

TAKE A DOG OUTSIDE TO PEE TWICE DURING THE NIGHT, BUT GET TO SLEEP IN?

POINTS: _____ I/10

WOULD YOU RATHER

GET LICKED BY 10 SLOBBERY PUPPIES

GET SAT ON BY ONE LARGE DOG?

POINTS: _____1/10

WOULD YOU RATHER

PLAY IN THE SNOW WITH A POLAR BEAR

PLAY IN THE WATER WITH A SEAL?

POINTS: _____1/10

WOULD YOU RATHER

GALLOP LIKE A HORSE

HOP LIKE A FROG?

Q/15

POINTS: _____1/10

WOULD YOU RATHER

HAVE FANGS LIKE A SNAKE

CLAWS LIKE AN EAGLE?

Q/16

POINTS: _____1/10

WOULD YOU RATHER

HAVE TO WRESTLE A GRIZZLY BEAR

A GORILLA?

Q 17

POINTS: _____1/10

WOULD YOU RATHER

SEE A DINOSAUR

A SABER TOOTH TIGER?

Q 18

POINTS: _____1/10

WOULD YOU RATHER

COME FACE TO FACE WITH A TIGER

A CROCODILE?

Q 19

POINTS: _____ 1/10

WOULD YOU RATHER

FIND ONE HUNDRED SPIDERS

ONE LION?

Q 20

POINTS: _____ 1/10

END OF THE THIRD ROUND

AGNES RAMA

PLAYER NUMBER 1'S POINTS SCORED

POINTS ....

WOULD YOU RATHER?

ROUND 4
HOLIDAY
QUESTIONS

PLAYER 2 STARTS THE GAME

WOULD YOU RATHER

HUNT FOR EASTER EGGS

HIDE THEM?

Q/1

POINTS: _____ 1/10

WOULD YOU RATHER

BE A WITCH

A VAMPIRE?

Q/2

POINTS: _____ 1/10

WOULD YOU RATHER

BE A GHOST

A WITCH?

POINTS: _____1/10

WOULD YOU RATHER

GO TRICK OR TREATING AT HALLOWEEN

PASS OUT CANDY?

POINTS: _____1/10

WOULD YOU RATHER

BE THE EASTER BUNNY

SANTA CLAUS?

POINTS: _____ 1/10

WOULD YOU RATHER

GET ONE BIG CHRISTMAS GIFT

12 SMALL ONES?

POINTS: _____ 1/10

WOULD YOU RATHER

CELEBRATE CHRISTMAS WITH YOUR RELATIVES

WITH YOUR IMMEDIATE FAMILY?

Q7

POINTS: _____1/10

WOULD YOU RATHER

GET NO GIFTS

COAL IN YOUR STOCKING AT CHRISTMAS?

Q8

POINTS: _____1/10

WOULD YOU RATHER

ONLY BE ABLE TO CELEBRATE YOUR BIRTHDAY

ONLY BE ABLE TO CELEBRATE CHRISTMAS?

POINTS: _____ 1/10

WOULD YOU RATHER

GET CASH FOR CHRISTMAS?

GET GIFTS FOR CHRISTMAS?

POINTS: _____ 1/10

WOULD YOU RATHER

BUILD A SNOWMAN?

MAKE SNOW ANGELS?

POINTS: _____I/10

WOULD YOU RATHER

SPEND ALL DAY WATCHING CHRISTMAS MOVIES?

SPEND ALL DAY SLEDDING?

POINTS: _____I/10

WOULD YOU RATHER

EAT A GIANT CHOCOLATE BUNNY

A GIANT JELLY BEAN?

Q 13

POINTS: _____1/10

WOULD YOU RATHER

RIDE ON THE EASTER BUNNY'S BACK

ON HIS LONG EARS?

Q 14

POINTS: _____1/10

WOULD YOU RATHER

BE BEST FRIENDS WITH THE EASTER BUNNY

SANTA CLAUS?

POINTS: _____ 1/10

WOULD YOU RATHER

HAVE AN EXTRA WEEK OF MARCH BREAK

AN EXTRA 10 CHOCOLATE BUNNIES

POINTS: _____ 1/10

WOULD YOU RATHER

SHARE YOUR EASTER CHOCOLATES WITH YOUR FRIENDS

KEEP THEM ALL TO YOURSELF?

Q 17

POINTS: _____ 1/10

WOULD YOU RATHER

HAVE BRIGHT RED HAIR FOR VALENTINE'S DAY

GREEN FOR ST. PATRICK'S DAY?

Q 18

POINTS: _____ 1/10

WOULD YOU RATHER

GO ON A HEART HUNT

AN EGG HUNT?

POINTS: _____ /10

WOULD YOU RATHER

HAVE AN ICE-CREAM CONE WITH ANCHOVY TOPPINGS

SPAGHETTI WITH HEART-SHAPED CANDIES IN IT?

POINTS: _____ /10

END OF THE FOURTH ROUND

AGNES RAMA

PLAYER NUMBER 2'S POINTS SCORED

POINTS ....

WOULD YOU RATHER?

ROUND 5

CHALLENGING QUESTIONS

PLAYER 1 STARTS THE GAME

WOULD YOU RATHER

BE AN EXPERT AT EVERYTHING

HAVE ALL KNOWLEDGE?

Q1

POINTS: _____1/10

WOULD YOU RATHER

WIN THE NOBEL PEACE PRIZE
OR 5 MILLION DOLLARS?
WOULD YOU RATHER TRAVEL
100 YEARS IN THE PAST

100 YEARS IN THE FUTURE?

Q2

POINTS: _____1/10

WOULD YOU RATHER

GO TO JAIL FOR A YEAR

BE HOMELESS FOR A YEAR?

POINTS: _____ I/10

WOULD YOU RATHER

LIVE WITH SOMEONE YOU HATE

LIVE COMPLETELY ALONE?

POINTS: _____ I/10

WOULD YOU RATHER

BE RICH WITH NO FRIENDS

POOR WITH LOTS OF GOOD FRIENDS?

POINTS: _____1/10

WOULD YOU RATHER

NEVER TOUCH AN ELECTRONIC DEVICE AGAIN

NEVER TOUCH A HUMAN AGAIN?

POINTS: _____1/10

WOULD YOU RATHER

HAVE A TERRIBLE SHORT-TERM MEMORY

FORGET EVERYTHING BAD THAT EVER HAPPENED TO YOU?

Q/7

POINTS: _____1/10

WOULD YOU RATHER

HAVE ONE WISH GRANTED TODAY

THREE WISHES GRANTED TEN YEARS FROM NOW?

Q/8

POINTS: _____1/10

WOULD YOU RATHER

BE HOMELESS AND HAVE FAMILY AND FRIENDS

LIVE COMFORTABLY BUT ENTIRELY ALONE?

POINTS: _____1/10

WOULD YOU RATHER

SPEND A WEEK ADRIFT AT SEA IN A LIFE RAFT

SPEND ONE MONTH IN THE COLDEST PLACE ON EARTH?

POINTS: _____1/10

WOULD YOU RATHER

SHARE A TOOTHBRUSH WITH A RANDOM STRANGER

KISS A RANDOM STRANGER ON THE MOUTH?

POINTS: _____ 1/10

WOULD YOU RATHER

BE ABLE TO EAT AS MUCH AS YOU WANT AND NEVER GAIN WEIGHT

FEEL REFRESHED AND WELL-RESTED AFTER ONLY THREE HOURS OF SLEEP EACH NIGHT?

POINTS: _____ 1/10

WOULD YOU RATHER

BE COMPLETELY ALONE FOR 5 YEARS

NEVER ALONE FOR 5 YEARS?

Q 13

POINTS: _____ 1/10

WOULD YOU RATHER

LOSE YOUR SENSE OF TASTE

YOUR SENSE OF SMELL?

Q 14

POINTS: _____ 1/10

WOULD YOU RATHER

NOT BE ABLE TO READ

NOT BE ABLE TO WRITE?

POINTS: _____1/10

WOULD YOU RATHER

HAVE TO EAT ONLY WARM FOOD

HAVE TO EAT ONLY COLD FOOD?

POINTS: _____1/10

WOULD YOU RATHER

SPEND 48 STRAIGHT HOURS IN A PUBLIC RESTROOM

THE SAME AMOUNT OF TIME IN A MORGUE?

POINTS: _____ 1/10

WOULD YOU RATHER

LIVE IN A PLACE WHERE IT IS ALWAYS COLD

IN A PLACE THAT IS ALWAYS HOT?

POINTS: _____ 1/10

WOULD YOU RATHER

SPEND A YEAR IN A HOSPITAL

A YEAR IN JAIL?

POINTS: _____ 1/10

WOULD YOU RATHER

TO BE THE GREATEST MAN ON EARTH

THE LOWEST ON EARTH

POINTS: _____ 1/10

END OF THE FIFTH ROUND

AGNES RAMA

PLAYER NUMBER 1'S POINTS SCORED

POINTS ....

WOULD YOU RATHER?

ROUND 6
HILARIOUS
QUESTIONS

PLAYER 2 STARTS THE GAME

WOULD YOU RATHER

BE SMALL ENOUGH TO FIT INSIDE A COMPUTER

A HUMAN BODY?

Q/1

POINTS: _____1/10

WOULD YOU RATHER

BE ABLE TO CONTROL THE WEATHER

UNDERSTAND WHAT ANIMALS ARE SAYING?

Q/2

POINTS: _____1/10

WOULD YOU RATHER

LIVE WITHOUT SWEETS

TV?

POINTS: _____ 1/10

WOULD YOU RATHER

HAVE YOUR PARENTS BE SECRET AGENTS

ALIENS?

POINTS: _____ 1/10

WOULD YOU RATHER

HAVE THE BEST LAUGH

THE BEST SMILE?

Q/5

POINTS: _____ 1/10

WOULD YOU RATHER

BE THE FUNNIEST AT SCHOOL

THE SMARTEST?

Q/6

POINTS: _____ 1/10

WOULD YOU RATHER

BE AN INSECT

A RODENT?

Q/7

POINTS: _____1/10

WOULD YOU RATHER

A SECRET AGENT

AN ALIEN?

Q/8

POINTS: _____1/10

WOULD YOU RATHER

LICK THE ROAD

THE SIDEWALK?

Q/9

POINTS: _____1/10

WOULD YOU RATHER

LOSE YOUR SENSE OF SMELL

SENSE OF TOUCH?

Q/10

POINTS: _____1/10

WOULD YOU RATHER

HAVE TO CLEAN A TOILET BOWL WITH YOUR TOOTHBRUSH

YOUR HAIR?

Q/11

POINTS: _____1/10

WOULD YOU RATHER

TAKE A BATH IN HONEY

HOT SAUCE?

Q/12

POINTS: _____1/10

WOULD YOU RATHER

BE TRAPPED IN A ROOM WITH 1 HUNGRY DINOSAUR

100 CRYING BABIES?

POINTS: _____ 1/10

WOULD YOU RATHER

BE STUNG BY 100 BEES

EAT 100 BEES?

POINTS: _____ 1/10

WOULD YOU RATHER

PASS GAS LOUDLY IN PUBLIC

POO, YOUR PANTS SILENTLY?

Q/15

POINTS: _____1/10

WOULD YOU RATHER

HAVE ALL THE MONEY IN THE WORLD

LIVE FOREVER?

Q/16

POINTS: _____1/10

WOULD YOU RATHER

BE A STAR

A PLANET?

Q/17

POINTS: _____1/10

WOULD YOU RATHER

HAVE TO SKIP EVERYWHERE

RUN?

Q/18

POINTS: _____1/10

WOULD YOU RATHER

HAVE NO KNEES

NO ELBOWS?

Q/19

POINTS: _____1/10

WOULD YOU RATHER

TO BE A NIGHT MAN

A DAY MAN?

Q/20

POINTS: _____1/10

END OF THE SIXTH ROUND

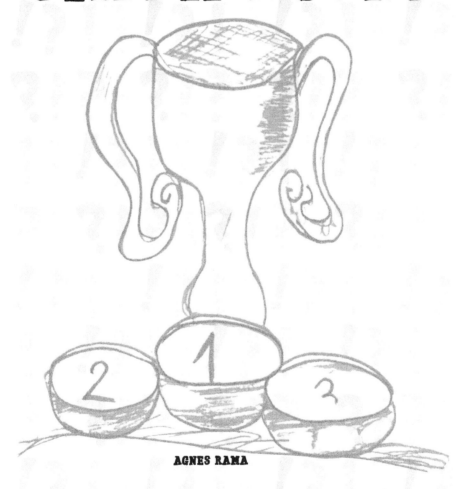

AGNES RAMA

PLAYER NUMBER 2'S POINTS SCORED

POINTS ....

WOULD YOU RATHER?

ROUND 7
HARDEST
QUESTIONS

PLAYER 1 STARTS THE GAME

WOULD YOU RATHER

ONLY BE ABLE TO WATCH MOVIES IN THE MOVIE THEATER

IN YOUR HOME FOR THE REST OF YOUR LIFE?

POINTS: _____1/10

WOULD YOU RATHER

ONLY BE ABLE TO DRINK APPLE JUICE

MILK FOR EVERY MEAL OF THE DAY?

POINTS: _____1/10

WOULD YOU RATHER

HAVE A TINY FRECKLE RIGHT IN THE MIDDLE OF YOUR FOREHEAD

ONE HUGE FRECKLE ON YOUR ARM?

POINTS: _____1/10

WOULD YOU RATHER

STAY YOUNG FOR AS LONG AS YOU LIVE

BE AN ADULT AS SOON AS YOU WERE BORN?

POINTS: _____1/10

WOULD YOU RATHER

DRIVE IN A POLICE CAR

IN A FIRE TRUCK?

Q/5

POINTS: _____1/10

WOULD YOU RATHER

HAVE TO RIDE A TRAIN TO GET EVERYWHERE

ALWAYS HAVE TO TAKE AN AIRPLANE?

Q/6

POINTS: _____1/10

WOULD YOU RATHER

BE THE TALLEST PERSON IN THE WORLD

THE SHORTEST PERSON IN THE WORLD?

POINTS: _____ I/10

WOULD YOU RATHER

MAKE 1,000 DOLLARS A DAY BUT NEVER SEE YOUR FAMILY

MAKE 10 DOLLARS A DAY AND ALWAYS BE ABLE TO SEE YOUR FAMILY?

POINTS: _____ I/10

WOULD YOU RATHER

ALWAYS SEE THE WORLD IN BLACK AND WHITE

ALWAYS SEE THE WORLD IN COLOR BUT WITH STRIPES?

POINTS: _____1/10

WOULD YOU RATHER

ALWAYS BE DRESSED UP IN YOUR FANCIEST CLOTHES

ALWAYS BE DRESSED UP IN YOUR DIRTIEST CLOTHES?

POINTS: _____1/10

WOULD YOU RATHER

BE ABLE TO PLAY ANY NEW VIDEO GAME THAT COMES OUT

OR

BE ABLE TO GET THE LATEST NEW PHONE WHEN IT COMES OUT?

POINTS: _____ I/10

WOULD YOU RATHER

BUY YOUR OWN AMUSEMENT PARK LIKE DISNEY

OR

BUY YOUR OWN PRIVATE ISLAND?

POINTS: _____ I/10

WOULD YOU RATHER

HAVE WATER THAT TASTES LIKE YOUR FAVORITE DRINK

VEGETABLES THAT TASTE LIKE YOUR FAVORITE DESSERT?

POINTS: _____1/10

WOULD YOU RATHER

ONLY BE ABLE TO SEE OUT OF ONE EYE

ONLY BE ABLE TO HEAR OUT OF ONE EAR?

POINTS: _____1/10

WOULD YOU RATHER

BE ABLE TO SPEAK TO ANY ANIMAL

KNOW EVERY LANGUAGE IN THE WORLD?

POINTS: _____1/10

WOULD YOU RATHER

BE ALL ALONE IN THE DESERT

IN THE JUNGLE?

Q 16

POINTS: _____1/10

WOULD YOU RATHER

ONLY BE ABLE TO WATCH ONE TV SHOW

HAVE TO WATCH ALL OF YOUR TV SHOWS IN BLACK AND WHITE?

POINTS: _____1/10

WOULD YOU RATHER

BE THE BEST PLAYER ON A WINNING TEAM

THE WORST PLAYER ON A LOSING TEAM?

POINTS: _____1/10

WOULD YOU RATHER

NEVER BE ABLE TO SEE YOUR GRANDPARENTS AGAIN

NEVER BE ABLE TO SEE YOUR BEST FRIENDS AGAIN?

Q/19

POINTS: _____ 1/10

WOULD YOU RATHER

BE ABLE TO SKIP ALL OF YOUR DENTIST APPOINTMENTS

ALL OF YOUR DOCTOR'S APPOINTMENTS?

Q/20

POINTS: _____ 1/10

END OF THE SEVENTH ROUND

AGNES RAMA

PLAYER NUMBER 1'S POINTS SCORED

POINTS ....

WOULD YOU RATHER?

ROUND 8
GROSS
QUESTIONS

PLAYER 2 STARTS THE GAME

WOULD YOU RATHER

HAVE TO EAT A CHILI-FLAVORED WASP

A SUGAR-COATED CRICKET?

Q1

POINTS: _____1/10

WIN A HOT DOG EATING CONTEST

A CHEESEBURGER EATING CONTEST?

Q2

POINTS: _____1/10

WOULD YOU RATHER

HAVE TO SNEEZE EVERY 10 MINUTES

BURP EVERY 10 MINUTES?

POINTS: _____1/10

WOULD YOU RATHER

HAVE TO LICK A TRASHCAN

LAY ON A FLOOR THAT HAD MOLDY FOOD?

POINTS: _____1/10

WOULD YOU RATHER

HAVE TO SMELL A SKUNK EVERY MORNING

GO DO THE GARBAGE DUMP EVERY AFTERNOON?

POINTS: _____ 1/10

WOULD YOU RATHER

NEED TO USE A LITTER BOX TO USE THE BATHROOM

USE THE BATHROOM OUTDOORS?

POINTS: _____ 1/10

WOULD YOU RATHER

R HAVE TO TAKE A BATH DRENCHED IN HONEY

A SHOWER SPRAYED WITH STICKY SYRUP?

Q/7

POINTS: _____1/10

WOULD YOU RATHER

HAVE 100 COCKROACHES IN YOUR ROOM

HAVE TO EAT ONE COCKROACH?

Q/8

POINTS: _____1/10

WOULD YOU RATHER

HAVE HAIR COVERING YOUR ENTIRE BODY

HAVE FEATHERS COVERING YOUR BODY?

POINTS: _____ 1/10

WOULD YOU RATHER

MUNCH ON A GRAPE THAT HAD MOLD ON IT

DRINKS WATER THAT HAD MUCK WITHIN IT?

POINTS: _____ 1/10

WOULD YOU RATHER

HAVE TO SMELL YOUR ENTIRE FAMILY'S UNDERWEAR EVERY MORNING

THEIR SOCKS EVERY AFTERNOON?

POINTS: _____ 1/10

WOULD YOU RATHER

HAVE A HUGE PIECE OF GREEN SALAD STUCK IN YOUR TEETH O

A BOOGER STUCK IN YOUR NOSTRIL?

POINTS: _____ 1/10

WOULD YOU RATHER

NOT TAKE A BATH FOR ONE MONTH

NOT CHANGE YOUR CLOTHES FOR ONE MONTH?

Q 13

POINTS: _____ /10

WOULD YOU RATHER

DRINK A SMOOTHIE MADE OF CRUSHED BUGS

EAT A SNAIL THAT HAS BEEN CRUSHED?

Q 14

POINTS: _____ /10

WOULD YOU RATHER

POOP CANDY

PEE LEMONADE EVERY TIME YOU USED THE BATHROOM?

POINTS: _____1/10

WOULD YOU RATHER

HAVE TO POOP 10 TIMES EVERY DAY

HAVE DIARRHEA EVERY TIME YOU POOP?

POINTS: _____1/10

WOULD YOU RATHER

HAVE TO EAT SUPER SPICY FOOD

THE MOST BITTER FOOD IN THE ENTIRE WORLD?

Q/17

POINTS: _____1/10

WOULD YOU RATHER

HAVE A 30-FOOT ANACONDA

A STINKY ELEPHANT AS YOUR SCHOOL MASCOT?

Q/18

POINTS: _____1/10

WOULD YOU RATHER

HAVE 1000 AGGRESSIVE WASPS CHASING YOU

10 SUPER STINKY SKUNKS?

POINTS: _____ /10

WOULD YOU RATHER

FOREVER EAT YOUR LEAST FAVORITE FOOD

SOMEONE ELSE'S BOOGERS ONCE AT EVERY MEAL?

POINTS: _____ /10

END OF THE EIGHTH ROUND

AGNES RAMA

PLAYER NUMBER 2'S POINTS SCORED

POINTS ....

WOULD YOU RATHER?

ROUND 9
SPORTS
QUESTIONS

PLAYER NUMBER 1 STARTS THE GAME

WOULD YOU RATHER

BE THE BEST AT A SPORT NO ONE HAS HEARD OF

THE WORST AT A SPORT EVERYONE LOVES?

Q/1

POINTS: _____1/10

WOULD YOU RATHER

ALWAYS LOSE

NEVER PLAY?

Q/2

POINTS: _____1/10

WOULD YOU RATHER

RUN A MARATHON

BIKE THE TOUR DE FRANCE?

POINTS: _____I/10

WOULD YOU RATHER

BE ABLE TO JUMP THE LENGTH OF A FOOTBALL FIELD

AS HIGH AS A SKYSCRAPER?

POINTS: _____I/10

WOULD YOU RATHER

GO SURFING

GO SNOWBOARDING?

POINTS: _____1/10

WOULD YOU RATHER

BE A VERY FAST RUNNER

A VERY FAST SWIMMER?

POINTS: _____1/10

WOULD YOU RATHER

BE A VERY FAST RUNNER

A VERY FAST SWIMMER?

Q/7

POINTS: _____1/10

WOULD YOU RATHER

PLAY BASEBALL

BASKETBALL?

Q/8

POINTS: _____1/10

WOULD YOU RATHER

GET FARAWAY SEATS BUT ATTEND TEN GAMES

FIELD/COURTSIDE SEATS AND GO TO ONE GAME OF YOUR FAVORITE TEAM?

POINTS: _____I/10

WOULD YOU RATHER

PLAY GOLF

PLAY BADMINTON?

POINTS: _____I/10

WOULD YOU RATHER

BE A TENNIS PLAYER

A FOOTBALL PLAYER?

POINTS: _____I/10

WOULD YOU RATHER

BE THE WORST PLAYER ON A TEAM THAT ALWAYS WINS

THE BEST PLAYER ON A TEAM THAT ALWAYS LOSES?

POINTS: _____I/10

WOULD YOU RATHER

PLAY SOCCER

FOOTBALL?

POINTS: _____ 1/10

WOULD YOU RATHER

GO TO A PROFESSIONAL SPORTS GAME

PLAY IN A PROFESSIONAL SPORTS GAME?

POINTS: _____ 1/10

WOULD YOU RATHER

BE A TEAM PLAYER

SINGULAR STAR?

POINTS: _____I/10

WOULD YOU RATHER

FLY A KITE

RIDE ON A SCOOTER?

POINTS: _____I/10

WOULD YOU RATHER

GO ICE SKATING

TOBOGGANING?

POINTS: _____ 1/10

WOULD YOU RATHER

VOLLEYBALL

SKATEBOARD?

POINTS: _____ 1/10

WOULD YOU RATHER

HOCKEY

SNOWBOARD

POINTS: _____ I/10

WOULD YOU RATHER

SPORT

REST?

POINTS: _____ I/10

END OF THE NINTH ROUND

AGNES RAMA

PLAYER NUMBER 1'S POINTS SCORED
POINTS ....

WOULD YOU RATHER?

ROUND 10
FOOD
QUESTIONS

PLAYER NUMBER 2 STARTS THE GAME

WOULD YOU RATHER

DRINK HOT CHOCOLATE

JUICE?

Q/1

POINTS: _____ 1/10

WOULD YOU RATHER

EAT PIZZA

ICE CREAM AS YOUR OWN MEAL FOR THE REST OF YOUR LIFE?

Q/2

POINTS: _____ 1/10

WOULD YOU RATHER

SMELL LIKE ONIONS

GARLIC FOR THE REST OF YOUR LIFE?

POINTS: _____1/10

WOULD YOU RATHER

NEVER HAVE ICE CREAM

NEVER HAVE CANDY AGAIN FOR THE REST OF YOUR LIFE?

POINTS: _____1/10

WOULD YOU RATHER

ONLY BE ABLE TO EAT FOOD THAT IS RED

ONLY BE ABLE TO EAT FOOD THAT IS GREEN?

POINTS: _____ 1/10

WOULD YOU RATHER

SMELL LIKE CHEESE

BROCCOLI?

POINTS: _____ 1/10

WOULD YOU RATHER

ONLY BE ABLE TO EAT BREAKFAST FOODS

DINNER FOODS FOR THE REST OF YOUR LIFE?

Q/7

POINTS: _____ I/10

WOULD YOU RATHER

ONLY WEAR CLOTHES DECORATED WITH PICTURES OF HAMBURGERS

PICTURES OF CANDY?

Q/8

POINTS: _____ I/10

WOULD YOU RATHER

EAT ONE GIANT MEAL PER DAY

TEN TINY MEALS PER DAY?

Q/9

POINTS: _____ /10

WOULD YOU RATHER

EAT ONLY VEGETABLES

ONLY FRUIT FOR THE REST OF YOUR LIFE?

Q/10

POINTS: _____ /10

WOULD YOU RATHER

BE AN EXPERT PASTRY CHEF AT A BAKERY

OR

AN EXPERT CHEF AT A FANCY RESTAURANT?

POINTS: _____ 1/10

WOULD YOU RATHER

ONLY BE ABLE TO EAT FOODS THAT GROW FROM THE EARTH

OR

ONLY BE ABLE TO EAT FOODS THAT ARE BAKED WITH FLOUR?

POINTS: _____ 1/10

WOULD YOU RATHER

ONLY EAT FOODS THAT LOOK DISGUSTING

SMELL DISGUSTING?

POINTS: _____ I/10

WOULD YOU RATHER

HAVE TO TAKE ONE BITE EVERY DAY OF THE STINKIEST CHEESE

A FRESH SNAIL FROM THE OCEAN?

POINTS: _____ I/10

WOULD YOU RATHER

ONLY USE MAPLE SYRUP

ONLY USE HONEY ON YOUR MEALS FOR THE REST OF YOUR LIFE?

POINTS: _____I/10

WOULD YOU RATHER

EAT ONLY PINK FOODS

ONLY BLUE FOODS?

POINTS: _____I/10

WOULD YOU RATHER

EAT DOG FOOD

CAT FOOD?

Q/17

POINTS: _____1/10

WOULD YOU RATHER

EAT DONUTS

CANDY EVERY DAY?

Q/18

POINTS: _____1/10

WOULD YOU RATHER

HAVE AN ICE CREAM CAKE

OR

A BAKERY CAKE?

Q/19

POINTS: _____ / 10

WOULD YOU RATHER

EAT ONLY CHOCOLATE

OR

ONLY VANILLA FOOD?

Q/20

POINTS: _____ / 10

END OF THE TENTH ROUND

PLAYER NUMBER 2'S POINTS SCORED

POINTS ....

WOULD YOU RATHER?

WE SUM UP THE PLAYERS' POINTS

PLAYER 1
POINTS........NAME.................................

PLAYER 2
POINTS........NAME.................................

GAME WINNER

PLAYER NUMBER..........
NAME.................................

A SPECIAL BONUS OF 56 KNOCK-KNOCK JOKES

1. Knock, Knock.

Who's there?

Scooby.

Scooby who?

Scooby doo of course!

2. Knock, Knock.

Who's there?

Dishes.

Dishes who?

Dishes the police, open up!

3. Knock, Knock.

Who's there?

Moustache.

Mustache who?

4. Knock, Knock.

Who's there?

Tank.

Tank who?

You're welcome!

5. Knock, Knock.

Who's there?

Kanga.

Kanga who?

Actually, it's a kangaroo!

6. Knock, Knock.

Who's there?

Radio.

Radio who?

Radio not, here I come!

7. Knock, Knock.

Who's there?

Razor.

Razor who?

Razor your hand if you have a question!

8. Knock, Knock.

Who's there?

Yah.

Yah who?

No silly – I prefer Google!

9. Knock, Knock.

Who's there?

Bacon.

Bacon who?

Baking some cookies in there? It smells delicious!

11. Knock, Knock.

Who's there?

Water.

Water who?

Water you doing? Just open the door!

13. Knock, Knock.

Who's there?

Boo.

Boo who?

Hey, don't cry!

15. Knock, Knock.

Who's there?

Doris.

Doris who?

Door is locked, that's why I'm knocking!

10. Knock, Knock.

Who's there?

Cow says.

Cow says who?

No, a cow says mooooo!

12. Knock, Knock.

Who's there?

Luke.

Luke who?

Luke through the peep hole and find out!

14. Knock, Knock.

Who's there?

Tritan.

Tritan who?

Tritan tell you a joke here!

16. Knock, Knock.

Who's there?

Snow.

Snow who?

Snow use. I forgot my name again!

17. Knock, Knock.

Who's there?

Jess.

Jess who?

Jess me, myself and I!

18. Knock, Knock.

Who's there?

Olive.

Olive who?

Olive next door. Hi neighbour!

19. Knock, Knock.

Who's there?

Turnip.

Turnip who?

Turnip the volume. I love this song!

20. Knock, Knock.

Who's there?

Theodore.

Theodore who?

Theodore won't open, so I knocked instead!

21. Knock, Knock.

Who's there?

Juno.

Juno who?

Juno how funny this is?

22. Knock, Knock.

Who's there?

Watts.

Watts who?

Watts for dinner? I'm starving!

23. Knock, Knock.

Who's there?

Broken pencil.

Broken pencil who?

Never mind, there's no point!

24. Knock, Knock.

Who's there?

Dozen.

Dozen who?

Dozen anybody want to let me in?

25. Knock, Knock.

Who's there?

Hatch.

Hatch who?

Bless you!

26. Knock, Knock.

Who's there?

Cargo.

Cargo who?

Cargo beep, beep and vroom, vroom!

27. Knock, Knock.

Who's there?

A herd.

A herd who?

A herd you were home. Can I come in please?

28. Knock, Knock.

Who's there?

Annie.

Annie who?

Annie way you can let me in?

29. Knock, Knock.

Who's there?

Hawaii.

Hawaii who?

I'm fine, Hawaii you?

30. Knock, Knock.

Who's there?

Amos.

Amos who?

A mosquito. Bzzzzz!

31. Knock, Knock.

Who's there?

Howard.

Howard who?

Howard I know?

32. Knock, Knock.

Who's there?

Goat.

Goat who?

Goat to the door and find out!

33. Knock, Knock.

Who's there?

Wood.

Wood who?

Would you care for another joke?

34. Knock, Knock.

Who's there?

Donut.

Donut who?

Donut ask, it's top secret!

35. Knock, Knock.

Who's there?

Gorilla.

Gorilla who?

Gorilla me a hamburger please!

36. Knock, Knock.

Who's there?

Who.

Who who?

Is there an owl in here?

37. Knock, Knock.

Who's there?

Banana.

Banana who?

Banana split!

38. Knock, Knock.

Who's there?

Weirdo.

Weirdo who?

Weirdo you think you're going?

39. Knock, Knock.

Who's there?

Broccoli.

Broccoli who?

Broccoli doesn't have a last name, silly!

40. Knock, Knock.

Who's there?

Nuisance.

Nuisance who?

What's new since yesterday?

41. Knock, Knock.

Who's there?

Lettuce.

Lettuce who?

Let us in – we're freezing!

42. Knock, Knock.

Who's there?

Alpaca.

Alpaca who?

Alpaca the suitcase and you load up the car!

43. Knock, Knock.

Who's there?

Barbie.

Barbie who?

Barbie-Q Chicken!

44. Knock, Knock.

Who's there?

Harry.

Harry who?

Harry up and answer the door!

45. Knock, Knock.

Who's there?

Urine.

Urine who?

Urine trouble if you don't answer the door!

46. Knock, Knock.

Who's there?

Figs.

Figs who?

Fix your doorbell, it's not working!

47. Knock, Knock.

Who's there?

Iran.

Iran who?

Iran all the way here. So let me in already!

48. Knock, Knock.

Who's there?

Will.

Will who?

Will you open the door please?

49. Knock, Knock.

Who's there?

Interrupting, squawking parrot.

Interrupting, squawking parr-

SQUAAAAAAAAWK!

50. Knock, Knock.

Who's there?

Barry.

Barry who?

Barry the treasure where no one will find it!

51. Knock, Knock.

Who's there?

Hal.

Hal who?

Hal, will you know if you don't open the door?

52. Knock, Knock.

Who's there?

Ben.

Ben who?

Ben knocking on this door all morning!

53. Knock, Knock.

Who's there?

Pecan.

Pecan who?

Hey! Pecan someone your own size!

54. Knock, Knock.

Who's there?

Mikey.

Mikey who?

Mikey doesn't fit in the keyhole! Help!

55. Knock, Knock.

Who's there?

Lena.

Lena who?

Lena a little closer, and I'll tell you another joke!

56. Knock, Knock.

Who's there?

Noah.

Noah who?

Noah anyone who can open this door?

We create our books with love and great care.
Your opinion will help us to improve this book and create new ones.

We love to hear from you.

Please, support us and leave a review!

Thank You! SCAN ME

Printed in Great Britain
by Amazon